# Key facts and fi...

## about Europe and the E...

# Contents

# The European Union – a success story

In many respects, the European Union (EU) is a remarkable success story. Over half a century, it has raised its citizens' standards of living to unprecedented levels. It has created a frontier-free single market and a single currency, the euro. It is a major economic power and the world leader in development aid. Its membership has grown from six to 25 nations, with two more set to join in 2007, bringing the EU's population to nearly half a billion.

Not all European countries are, or wish to be, EU members - but the Union welcomes membership applications from any democratic European country. It maintains close and friendly relations with all its neighbours, both in Europe and around the eastern and southern shores of the Mediterranean.

Though richly diverse, EU countries are united in their commitment to peace, democracy, the rule of law and respect for human rights. They seek to promote these values in the wider world, to build and share prosperity and to exert their collective influence by acting together on the world stage.

Using a variety of charts and facts and figures about the European Union and its member states, sometimes comparing them with other major economies. The countries that are candidates for EU membership are also included, but in a separate section.

For simplicity, some figures have been rounded up. An asterisk next to a figure means it is provisional or an estimate. The abbreviations used for the different countries are those shown in the key on page 6.

A great deal more information about the European Union is available via the Europa internet portal (**http://europa.eu.int**). For example, Eurostat (the EU's statistical office) publishes thousands of tables of detailed statistics on its website (**http://europa.eu.int/comm/eurostat**). You can access this data free of charge.

#  The European Union – a growing family

The EU began in the 1950s as the 'European Communities'. There were six member states: Belgium, Germany, France, Italy, Luxembourg and the Netherlands. They were joined by Denmark, Ireland and the United Kingdom in 1973, Greece in 1981, Spain and Portugal in 1986. Reunification of Germany in 1990 brought in the East German *Länder*.

In 1992, a new treaty gave new powers and responsibilities to the Community institutions and introduced new forms of cooperation between the member state governments, thus creating the European Union as such. The EU was enlarged in 1995 to include Austria, Finland and Sweden.

The 2004 enlargement brought in the Czech Republic, Estonia, Cyprus, Latvia, Lithuania, Hungary, Malta, Poland, Slovenia and Slovakia. Two more countries, Bulgaria and Romania, are on course to join in 2007. Two others, Croatia and Turkey, are also beginning negotiations for EU membership.

Europe has always been home to many different peoples and cultures. In every member state, a proportion of the population is made up of people from other countries - usually with close historical ties to the host country. The EU regards ethnic and cultural diversity as a great asset, and it promotes tolerance, respect and mutual understanding - values that Europe's long history has taught us.

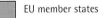 EU member states

 Candidate countries

2005

# Key

## EU members

**EU-25** ★ EU-25 means the 25 countries that are now EU members, taken together.

**EU-15** ★ EU-15 means the EU of 15 countries before its enlargement in 2004.

**BE** ☐ Belgium

**CZ** ☐ Czech Republic

**DK** ☐ Denmark

**DE** ■ Germany

**EE** ☐ Estonia

**EL** ☐ Greece

**ES** ☐ Spain

**FR** ☐ France

**IE** ☐ Ireland

**IT** ☐ Italy

**CY** ☐ Cyprus

**LV** ☐ Latvia

**LT** ☐ Lithuania

**LU** ☐ Luxembourg

**HU** ☐ Hungary

**MT** ■ Malta

**NL** ☐ Netherlands

**AT** ☐ Austria

**PL** ■ Poland

**PT** ☐ Portugal

**SI** ☐ Slovenia

**SK** ☐ Slovakia

**FI** ☐ Finland

**SE** ☐ Sweden

**UK** ■ United Kingdom

## Candidate countries

**BG** ☐ Bulgaria

**HR** ■ Croatia

**RO** ☐ Romania

**TR** ☐ Turkey

## Other countries

**CN** ★ China

**IN** ■ India

**JP** ◉ Japan

**RU** ☐ Russia

**US** ★ United States

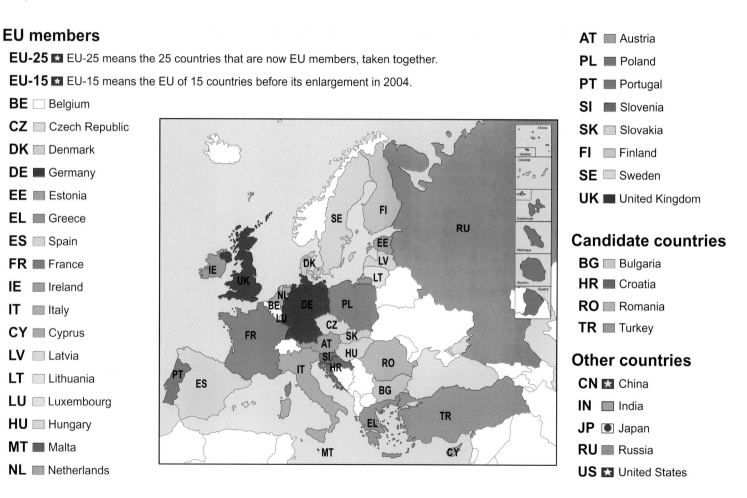

# Size and population

The European Union is only about two fifths the size of the United States, but its population is 57% larger. In fact, the EU population is the world's third largest after China and India.

Birth rates in the EU are falling and Europeans are living longer. These trends have important implications for the future.

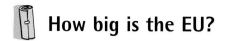 # How big is the EU?

The European Union covers nearly four million square kilometres. Seen on a map of the world, this is not a huge area – but it embraces 25 countries. Their size varies widely, from France (biggest) to Malta (smallest).

## Surface area in 2001, measured in thousands of square kilometres

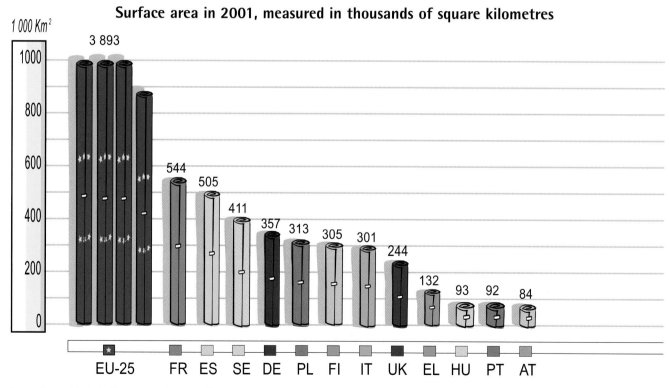

The figure for France does not include the overseas departments.

*Source*: Eurostat.

79 70 65 65 49 45 43 34 31 20 9 3 0.3

CZ IE LT LV SK EE DK NL BE SI CY LU MT

## Surface area, measured in millions of square kilometres

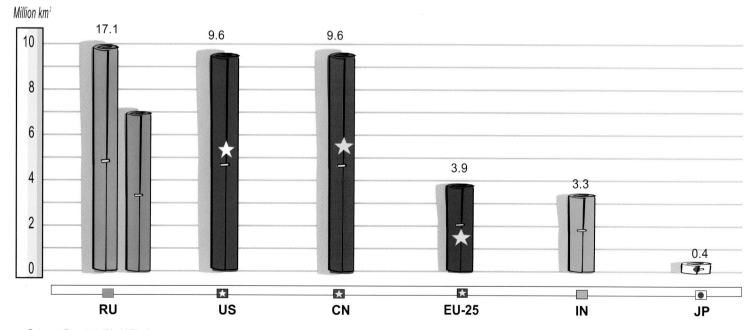

Million km²

| | RU | US | CN | EU-25 | IN | JP |
|---|---|---|---|---|---|---|
| | 17.1 | 9.6 | 9.6 | 3.9 | 3.3 | 0.4 |

Sources: Eurostat, World Bank.

# How many people live in the EU?

The European Union has about 457 million inhabitants - the world's third largest population after China and India.

The developed world's share of the world's population is shrinking - from 30% in 1960 to 19% in 2002. Four out of every five people on this planet now live in the developing world. This is a matter for real concern, and one reason why the EU is actively promoting global development. It is already the world's leading supplier of development aid.

## Population measured in millions of people

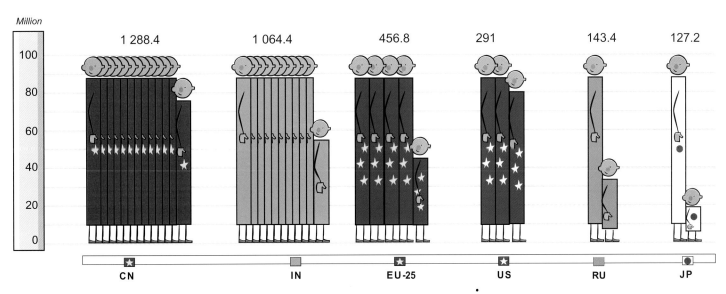

Figures for the EU-25 are for 2004, figures for the other countries are for mid-year 2003.

*Sources*: Eurostat, World Bank.

The EU's 457 million people are not spread evenly across the continent: some countries (and some regions) are more densely populated than others. This explains why the order of size of the countries is not always the same as the order of size of their populations.

**Population on 1 January 2004, measured in millions of people**

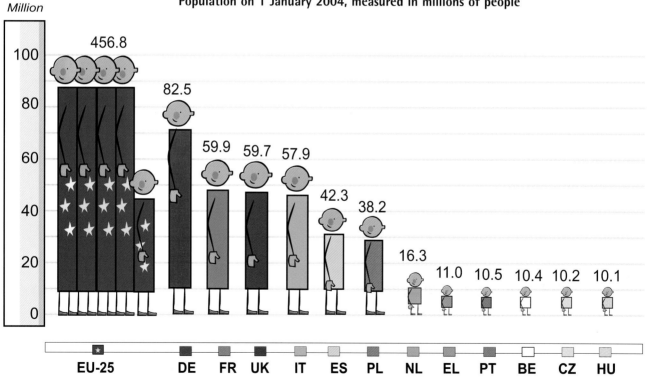

*Source*: Eurostat.

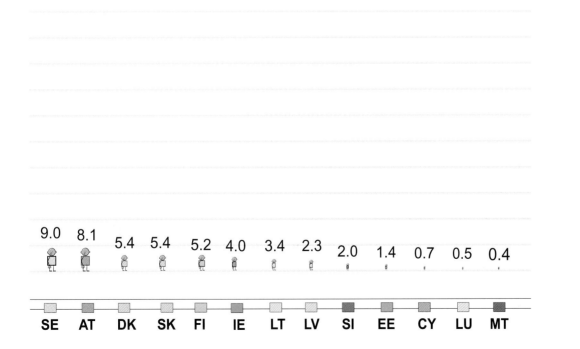

| 9.0 | 8.1 | 5.4 | 5.4 | 5.2 | 4.0 | 3.4 | 2.3 | 2.0 | 1.4 | 0.7 | 0.5 | 0.4 |
|-----|-----|-----|-----|-----|-----|-----|-----|-----|-----|-----|-----|-----|
| SE | AT | DK | SK | FI | IE | LT | LV | SI | EE | CY | LU | MT |

# Europeans are getting older

Europeans are living longer. Babies born in 1960 could be expected to survive to the age of about 67 (men) and 73 (women). Babies born in 2002 are expected to live much longer - till they are nearly 75 (men) and over 81 (women).

By way of comparison, figures from the United Nations show that babies born between 2000 and 2005 in Somalia, one of the world's least developed countries, are only expected to live until the age of 46 (men) and 49 (women).

**Life expectancy at birth, men and women in the EU-25, 1962-2002**

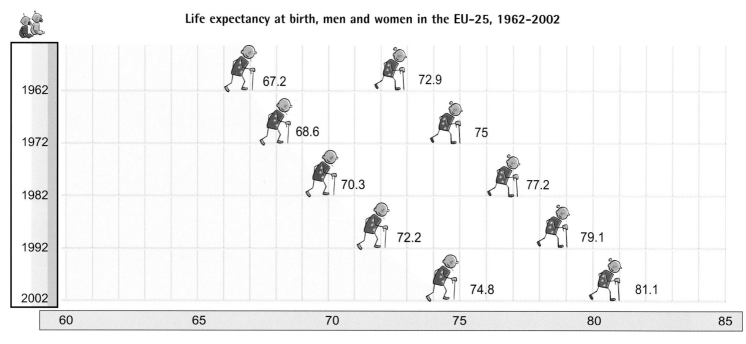

All figures are estimates.

*Source*: Eurostat.

Forty years ago, women in the EU-25 could be expected (on average) to have more than 2.5 children in their lifetime. But birth rates have been falling in Europe: women can now be expected to have (on average) less than 1.5 children. With fewer and fewer young people in the EU, the workforce is shrinking. This shrinking workforce has to support more and more pensioners, as the graph below shows.

To maintain or increase the size of its working population, Europe needs a combination of skilled immigration, lifelong learning, more women in work and more people working part-time beyond retirement age. More babies would also help!

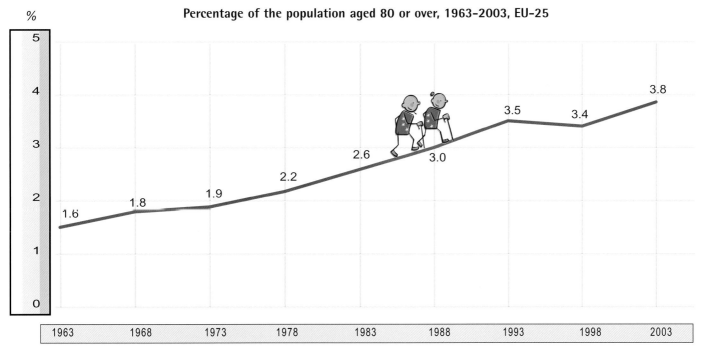

**Percentage of the population aged 80 or over, 1963–2003, EU-25**

%

5 — 
4 — 3.8
3 — 3.5   3.4
       3.0
   2.6
   2.2
   1.9
 1.8
1.6
1 — 
0 — 

1963  1968  1973  1978  1983  1988  1993  1998  2003

*Source*: Eurostat.

 # Europe: a new place to call home

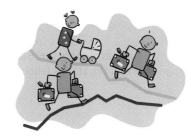

Europe's population increases through a combination of **natural growth** (i.e. more people are born than die) and **net migration** (i.e. more people settle in the EU than leave it).

Today, most of the EU's total population growth is due to net migration. Indeed, without immigration, the population of Germany, Greece and Italy would have fallen in 2003. Immigration brings much-needed young people into the EU workforce.

**Total population growth (blue line) and net migration (red line) in the EU-25, per 1 000 inhabitants, 1992–2003**

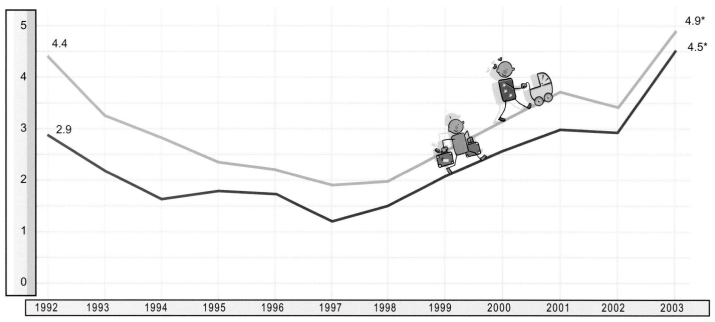

*Source*: Eurostat.

Europe has a long tradition of hospitality and of giving refuge to people fleeing war or persecution in the world's troubled areas. The number of asylum seekers increases in times of war, such as during the Balkan conflicts in the early 1990s. The number of asylum applications in the EU has fallen since those days and in 2002 it was no higher than in 1990.

**Number of asylum applications, in thousands, in the EU–25, 1990–2002**

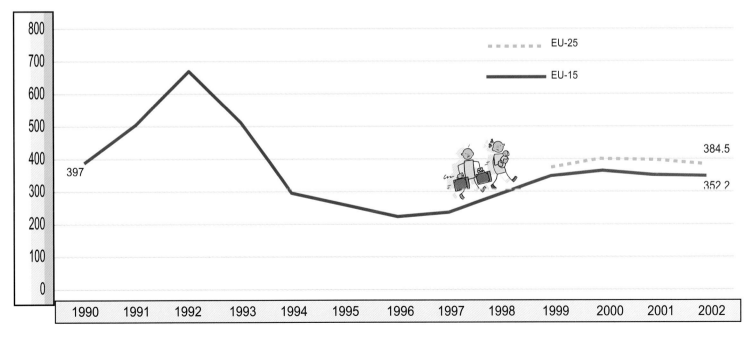

*Source*: Eurostat.

# Quality of life

A good quality of life depends on a whole series of factors, including having enough money and being in good health. How wealthy and healthy are Europeans? The answer varies from one country to another.

To get a rough idea of the material standard of living in a particular country we can measure the total value of everything that country produces in a given calendar year (its 'gross domestic product': GDP) and then divide that figure by the number of inhabitants.

But prices vary from one country to another, and those price differences must be eliminated before we can compare standards of living. We can do this by measuring the price of a comparable and representative 'basket' of goods and services in each country. This figure is given not in national currency units but in a common artificial currency we call the **'purchasing power standard'** (PPS).

Comparing GDP per inhabitant in PPS gives a fair comparison of the standard of living in different countries.

# How wealthy are Europeans?

Standards of living in Europe have improved significantly over the past decade. In 1995, GDP per inhabitant (in PPS) for the EU-25 was 15 200. Eight years later it had risen to 21 400.

In European countries, standards of living are among the highest in the world.

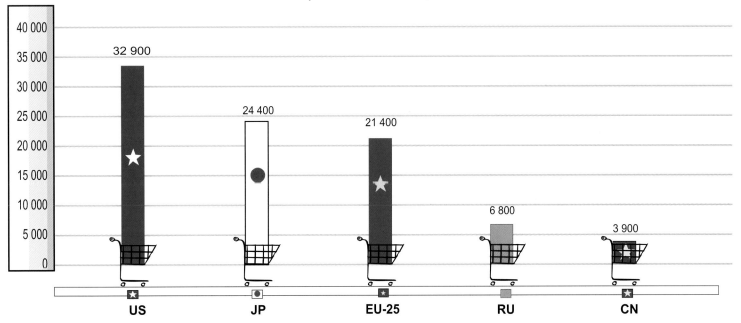

**GDP per inhabitant in PPS, 2003**

| | | |
|---|---|---|
| 40 000 | | |
| 35 000 | 32 900 (US) | |
| 30 000 | | |
| 25 000 | 24 400 (JP) | |
| 20 000 | 21 400 (EU-25) | |
| 15 000 | | |
| 10 000 | | |
| 5 000 | 6 800 (RU) | 3 900 (CN) |
| 0 | | |

US   JP   EU-25   RU   CN

Figures for Russia and China are for 2001.

*Source*: Eurostat.

The standard of living in the EU varies from country to country. GDP per inhabitant (in PPS) is highest in Luxembourg and lowest in Latvia. The EU is striving to strengthen the EU's economy, make it more competitive and create more jobs so we can all enjoy a better quality of life.

**GDP per inhabitant in PPS, 2003**

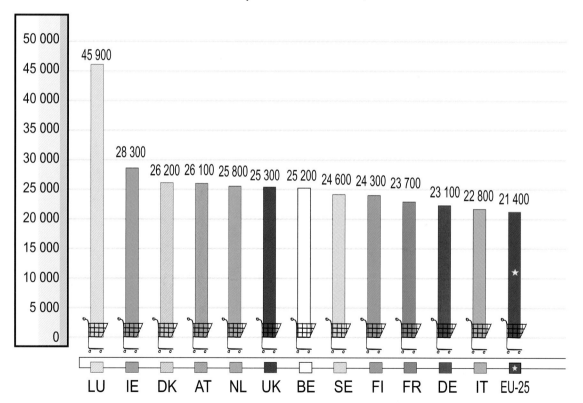

Source: Eurostat.

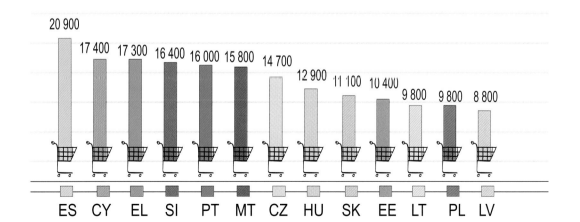

| ES | CY | EL | SI | PT | MT | CZ | HU | SK | EE | LT | PL | LV |
|----|----|----|----|----|----|----|----|----|----|----|----|----|
| 20 900 | 17 400 | 17 300 | 16 400 | 16 000 | 15 800 | 14 700 | 12 900 | 11 100 | 10 400 | 9 800 | 9 800 | 8 800 |

Standards of living also vary within each country. In some regions of the EU, as the map shows, GDP per inhabitant in PPS is less than 50% of the EU-25 average. In other regions it is 25% higher than the EU-25 average.

The EU's Structural Funds help even out these differences by improving life in poorer regions. Over 35% of the EU's budget is used to boost the economies of these regions, and in turn strengthen the EU as a whole.

**GDP per inhabitant in PPS as a percentage of the EU-25 average, 2002**

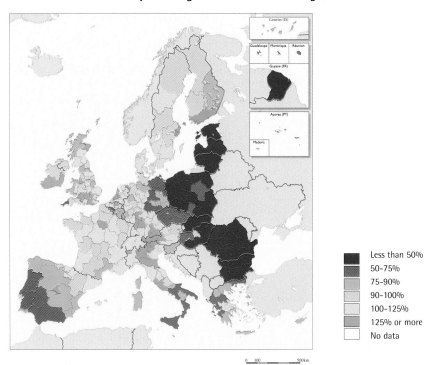

Less than 50%
50-75%
75-90%
90-100%
100-125%
125% or more
No data

The figures represent the data available as of 25 January 2005. Figures for French overseas departments refer to 2000.

*Source*: European Commission.

# How healthy are Europeans?

Smoking, poor diet and lack of exercise are among the factors that increase your risk of developing cancer and ischaemic heart disease - in which clogged or damaged arteries deliver too little blood to the heart.

Interestingly, more men than women die of these diseases in the EU, and the proportion of the population affected varies widely from one Member State to another. In 2000, Hungary had the highest death rate from cancer, while for ischaemic heart diseases it was Estonia. The death rate from cancer was lowest in Finland, while France reported the EU's lowest death rate for ischaemic heart diseases.

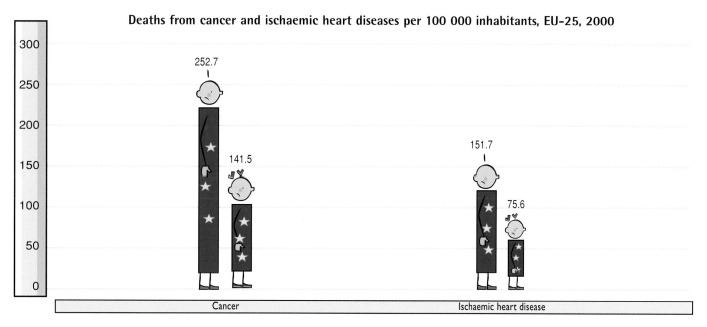

**Deaths from cancer and ischaemic heart diseases per 100 000 inhabitants, EU-25, 2000**

Cancer: 252.7, 141.5
Ischaemic heart disease: 151.7, 75.6

*Source*: Eurostat.

Sport is good for health. A Eurobarometer survey carried out in late 2004 indicates that 38% of people in the EU engage in some sporting activity at least once a week. The percentage in each country varies: it is highest in Scandinavia and lowest in some southern countries such as Portugal and some new member states such as Hungary.

But there are exceptions to the old-new divide: for example, Slovenians appear to be very physically active.

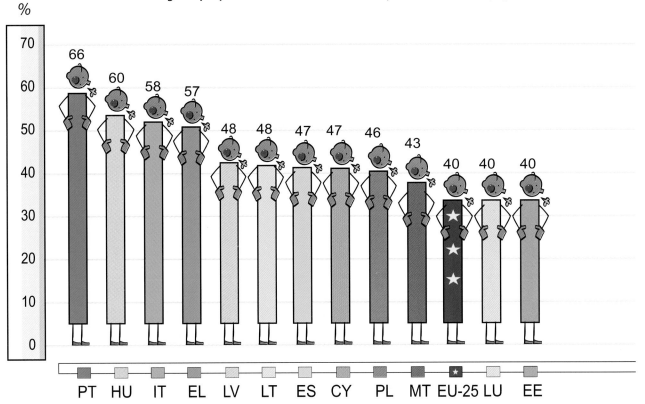

**Percentage of people interviewed in each country who never do any sport, 2004**

| PT | HU | IT | EL | LV | LT | ES | CY | PL | MT | EU-25 | LU | EE |
|----|----|----|----|----|----|----|----|----|----|-------|----|----|
| 66 | 60 | 58 | 57 | 48 | 48 | 47 | 47 | 46 | 43 | 40 | 40 | 40 |

*Source*: Eurobarometer.

Overall, more men than women go in for sports, and the younger you are the more physically active you are likely to be.

The graph shows the percentage of people interviewed in each EU country who say they never do any sports.

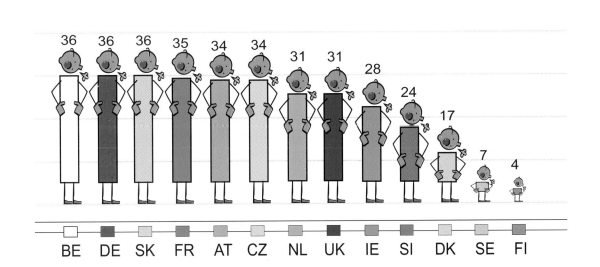

| BE | DE | SK | FR | AT | CZ | NL | UK | IE | SI | DK | SE | FI |
|----|----|----|----|----|----|----|----|----|----|----|----|----|
| 36 | 36 | 36 | 35 | 34 | 34 | 31 | 31 | 28 | 24 | 17 | 7 | 4 |

# 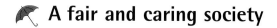 A fair and caring society

The European social model takes different forms in different countries, but all EU countries aim to be fair and caring societies. Tax revenue helps pay for social protection systems (such as pension, healthcare and unemployment benefit schemes) which are designed to protect vulnerable members of society. The amount of money spent on each inhabitant varies from country to country.

As the population ages, those in work have to support an increasing number of senior citizens. To take account of this trend, and to keep welfare costs under control, EU countries are redesigning their social protection systems. Europe's social model has to be modernised to preserve it for future generations.

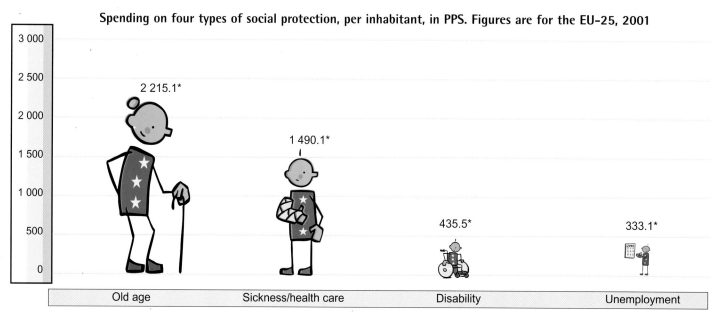

**Spending on four types of social protection, per inhabitant, in PPS. Figures are for the EU-25, 2001**

2 215.1*

1 490.1*

435.5*

333.1*

| Old age | Sickness/health care | Disability | Unemployment |

*Source*: Eurostat.

# Education, research and the information society

The EU's ambition is to become the world's most dynamic knowledge-based economy. That means investing heavily in research (the source of new knowledge) and in education and training, which give people access to that new knowledge.

Particularly important is training the workforce in information technology skills - and easier, faster access to the internet for schools, businesses and people at home.

A thriving economy needs people to stay in work longer and to learn new skills throughout their working lives. 'Lifelong learning' is the watchword. In the EU, the number of adults on training courses has been rising - to reach 9.4% in 2004.

As it competes for economic success in the global marketplace, the European Union is up against tough rivals such as Japan and the United States.

 # Education: investing in people

Education is the key to success - for individuals and for the EU as a whole. How much of its wealth does each EU country spend on educating its people?

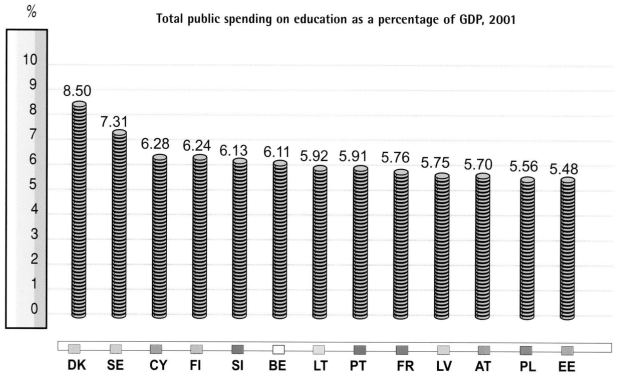

%

**Total public spending on education as a percentage of GDP, 2001**

| DK | SE | CY | FI | SI | BE | LT | PT | FR | LV | AT | PL | EE |
|------|------|------|------|------|------|------|------|------|------|------|------|------|
| 8.50 | 7.31 | 6.28 | 6.24 | 6.13 | 6.11 | 5.92 | 5.91 | 5.76 | 5.75 | 5.70 | 5.56 | 5.48 |

DK: figures do not include post-secondary non-tertiary education.
FR: figures do not include French overseas departments.
CY: figures include financial aid to students studying abroad.
LU: figures do not include tertiary education.
PT: figures do not include local government expenditure.

*Source*: Eurostat.

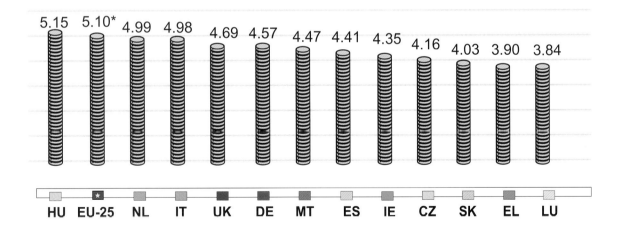

| HU | EU-25 | NL | IT | UK | DE | MT | ES | IE | CZ | SK | EL | LU |
|------|--------|------|------|------|------|------|------|------|------|------|------|------|
| 5.15 | 5.10* | 4.99 | 4.98 | 4.69 | 4.57 | 4.47 | 4.41 | 4.35 | 4.16 | 4.03 | 3.90 | 3.84 |

Education beyond the minimum school leaving age - and especially at university level - is the key to a satisfying career for many people, and is essential in giving the EU a well-qualified workforce. The good news is that, in most EU countries, more and more 18-year-olds are studying.

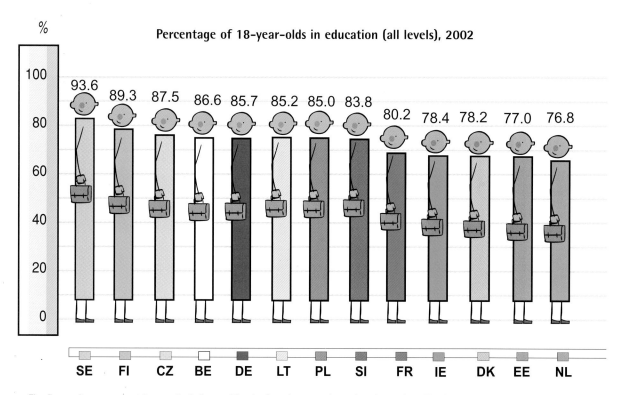

**Percentage of 18-year-olds in education (all levels), 2002**

The figures for some countries may be influenced by the fact that secondary education ends earlier than in other countries.
BE: figures do not include independent private institutions.
CY and LU: most students study abroad and are not included.
UK: population data is for 2001.

*Source*: Eurostat.

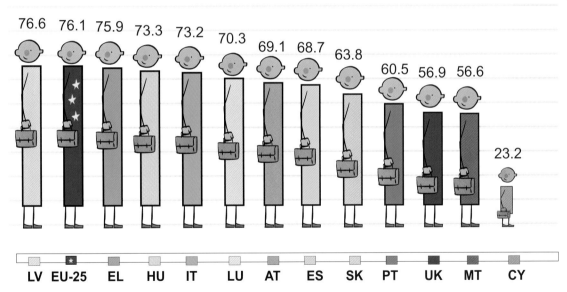

| LV | EU-25 | EL | HU | IT | LU | AT | ES | SK | PT | UK | MT | CY |
|----|-------|----|----|----|----|----|----|----|----|----|----|----|
| 76.6 | 76.1 | 75.9 | 73.3 | 73.2 | 70.3 | 69.1 | 68.7 | 63.8 | 60.5 | 56.9 | 56.6 | 23.2 |

# What subjects do Europeans study?

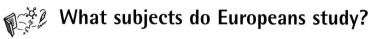

Women, whose educational attainments were below men's in Europe a generation ago, have now caught up. In 2001, more women than men graduated from higher education in the EU. The subjects Europeans choose to study tend to differ according to their gender: more men choose science, computing and engineering; more women choose the arts, humanities and law.

Europe needs well-qualified people in all walks of life. In particular, it needs more women in professional careers, and more scientists (of both genders) to carry out vital research.

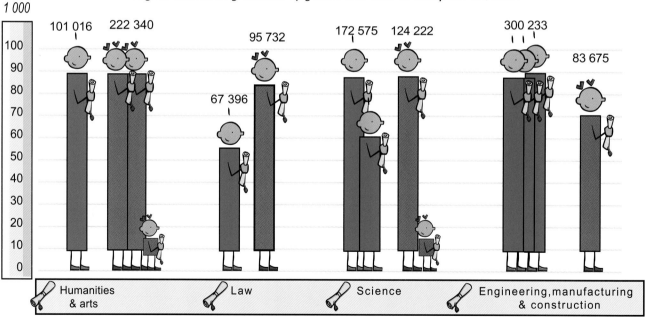

### Higher education graduates by gender and field of study, EU-25, 2001

*1 000*

101 016 · 222 340 · 95 732 · 67 396 · 172 575 · 124 222 · 300 233 · 83 675

Humanities & arts · Law · Science · Engineering, manufacturing & construction

*Source*: Eurostat.

# Better education means better job prospects

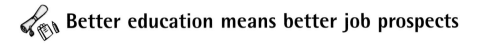

On the whole, the less educated you are, the more likely you are to be unemployed. If you have completed 'tertiary' education (e.g. a university degree course), you are more than twice as likely to have a job as someone with only primary or lower secondary schooling.

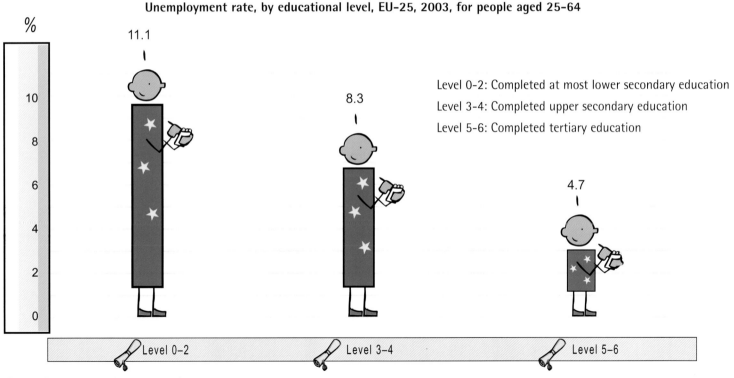

**Unemployment rate, by educational level, EU-25, 2003, for people aged 25-64**

%

11.1

8.3

4.7

Level 0-2: Completed at most lower secondary education

Level 3-4: Completed upper secondary education

Level 5-6: Completed tertiary education

Level 0-2

Level 3-4

Level 5-6

*Sources*: Eurostat, labour force survey, spring.

# Information technology: an essential tool

All over the EU, more and more firms and households are getting connected to the internet, and more business is being done online - which boosts efficiency. In 2004, 89% of businesses and 42% of households in the EU had access to the internet.

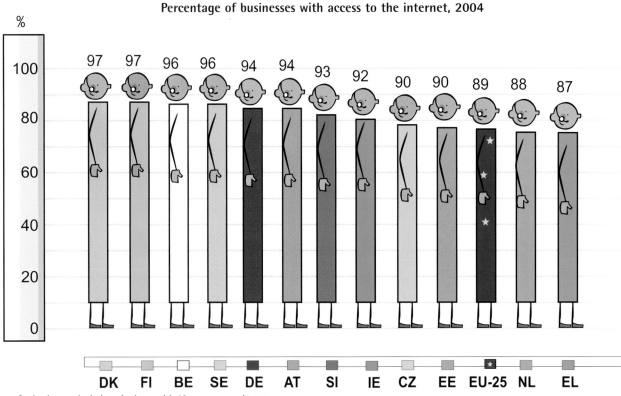

**Percentage of businesses with access to the internet, 2004**

%

DK 97 · FI 97 · BE 96 · SE 96 · DE 94 · AT 94 · SI 93 · IE 92 · CZ 90 · EE 90 · EU-25 89 · NL 88 · EL 87

The figures for businesses include only those with 10 or more employees.

Figures for FR and LU are for 2003.

*Source*: Eurostat.

However, this figure varies across the EU. For example, 69% of households in Denmark had access to the internet in 2004 while in Hungary this figure was only 14%. One of the EU's priorities is to ensure that all its citizens have fast, reliable access to the internet and the skills to handle information technology. The 'digital divide' between people in different countries and regions must be narrowed.

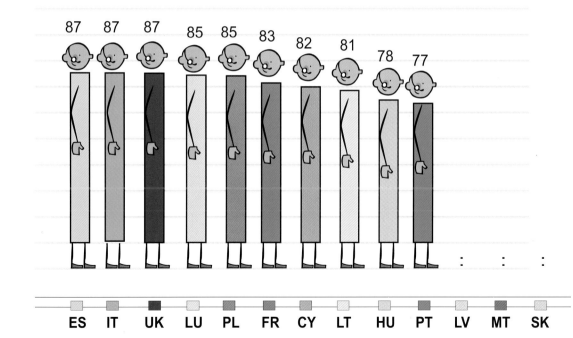

| ES | IT | UK | LU | PL | FR | CY | LT | HU | PT | LV | MT | SK |
|----|----|----|----|----|----|----|----|----|----|----|----|----|
| 87 | 87 | 87 | 85 | 85 | 83 | 82 | 81 | 78 | 77 |    |    |    |

# Research – key to the future

Research and development (R&D), especially in new technologies, holds the key to future competitiveness and jobs, which is why the EU's new strategy (since 2000) is to invest much more in research, rivalling the USA and Japan.

Although Japan's total investment in R&D is less than the EU's, Japan's research investment actually accounted for more than 3% of its GDP in 2001. The figure for the USA was 2.8%. The EU, which spent only 1.9% of its GDP on research in 2001, aims to boost this figure to 3% by 2010.

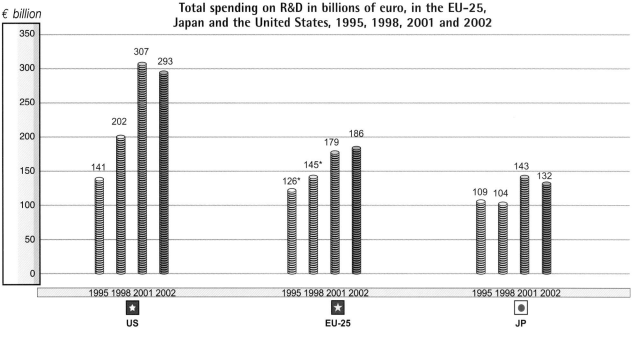

**Total spending on R&D in billions of euro, in the EU-25, Japan and the United States, 1995, 1998, 2001 and 2002**

€ billion

US: 141 (1995), 202 (1998), 307 (2001), 293 (2002)
EU-25: 126* (1995), 145* (1998), 179 (2001), 186 (2002)
JP: 109 (1995), 104 (1998), 143 (2001), 132 (2002)

Figures for the EU-25 do not include LU and MT.

*Sources*: Eurostat and OECD.

# Europeans at work

Employment is a top priority for the EU. In order to become the world's most dynamic and competitive economy, it must create more and better jobs for its citizens. It must also ensure equal opportunities, so that everyone who wants to can work. The aim is to achieve an employment rate of 70% by 2010.

 # How many people work in the EU?

In 2003, 63% of people of working age in the EU-25 had jobs. However, the employment rate varies across the EU. It is also different for men and women.

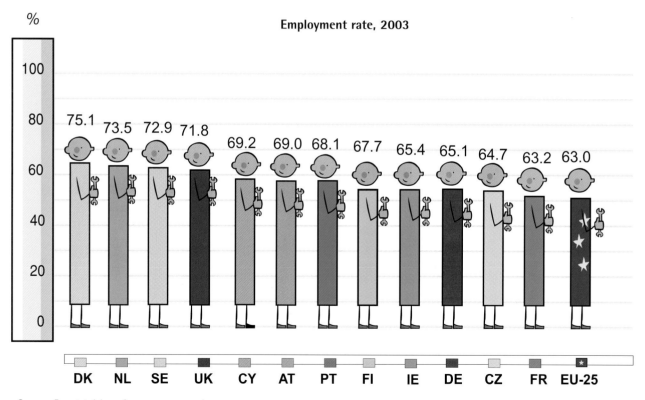

**Employment rate, 2003**

| DK | NL | SE | UK | CY | AT | PT | FI | IE | DE | CZ | FR | EU-25 |
|---|---|---|---|---|---|---|---|---|---|---|---|---|
| 75.1 | 73.5 | 72.9 | 71.8 | 69.2 | 69.0 | 68.1 | 67.7 | 65.4 | 65.1 | 64.7 | 63.2 | 63.0 |

*Sources*: Eurostat, labour force survey, annual average.

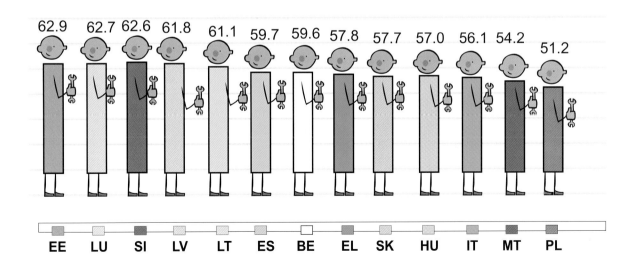

| 62.9 | 62.7 | 62.6 | 61.8 | 61.1 | 59.7 | 59.6 | 57.8 | 57.7 | 57.0 | 56.1 | 54.2 | 51.2 |
|------|------|------|------|------|------|------|------|------|------|------|------|------|
| EE | LU | SI | LV | LT | ES | BE | EL | SK | HU | IT | MT | PL |

Tackling unemployment is vital for the EU. The unemployment rate varies from one country and region to another. In 2003, the lowest level of unemployment was in Bolzano/Bozen (northern Italy), while the highest rate was 31.8% on the island of Réunion (part of France).

Overall, 9.0% of the EU's labour force was unemployed in summer 2004, compared with 5.4% in the United States.

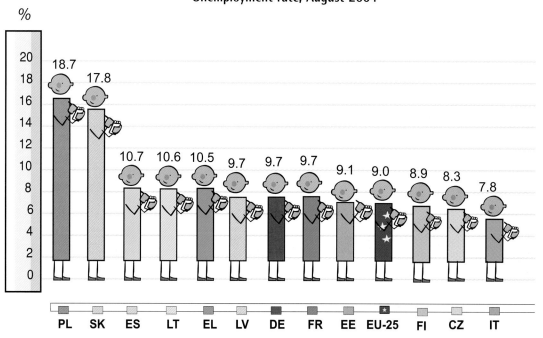

**Unemployment rate, August 2004**

EL: figures are for April to June 2004.
IT: figures are for July to September 2004.
*Source*: Eurostat.

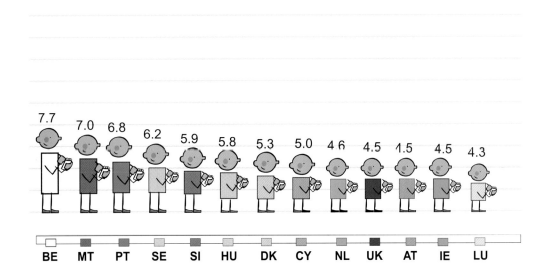

| BE | MT | PT | SE | SI | HU | DK | CY | NL | UK | AT | IE | LU |
|----|----|----|----|----|----|----|----|----|----|----|----|----|
| 7.7 | 7.0 | 6.8 | 6.2 | 5.9 | 5.8 | 5.3 | 5.0 | 4.6 | 4.5 | 4.5 | 4.5 | 4.3 |

# The jobs people do

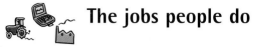

In the 1950s, over 20% of people in the EU (only six countries at the time) worked in farming and around 40% in industry. By 2003, those figures had dropped to 5.2% and 25.5% for the EU-25.

Meanwhile, the services sector has been growing fast and it now employs more than two thirds of the EU's workforce.

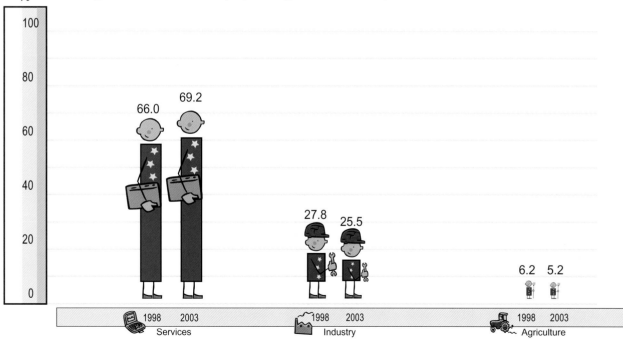

**% Percentage of the workforce employed in agriculture, industry and services, EU-25, 1998 and 2003**

*Sources*: Eurostat, national accounts, annual average.

# Equal opportunities for all?

In each age bracket, more men than women have jobs in the EU. This is sometimes due to discrimination in the workplace, sometimes the result of personal choice or cultural traditions.

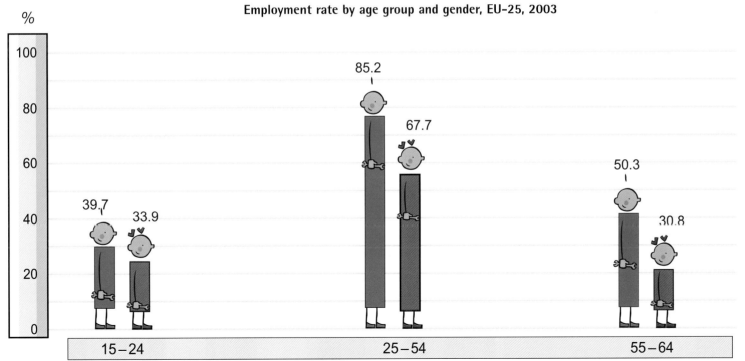

**Employment rate by age group and gender, EU–25, 2003**

%

100

80

60

40

20

0

39.7  33.9

85.2  67.7

50.3  30.8

15–24          25–54          55–64

*Sources*: Eurostat, labour force survey, annual average.

In all EU countries, women earn (on average) less than men. This 'gender pay gap' is widest in Cyprus, where women earned 26% less than men in 2001. It is narrowest (6%) in Italy. If the EU is to increase the size of its working population, better pay and conditions are needed to attract more women into the labour market.

The EU must also keep people of both genders working longer. It is making a special effort to help people of all ages to find jobs and keep them. That includes policies to encourage part-time work and to remove conflicts between career and private life.

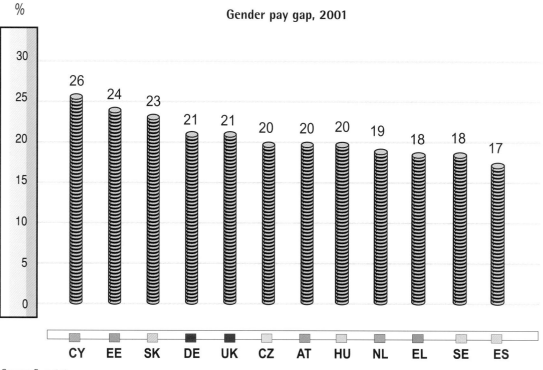

**Gender pay gap, 2001**

*Source*: Eurostat.

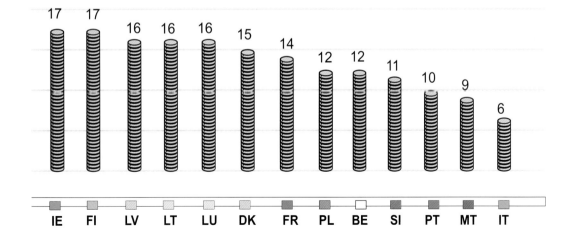

| 17 | 17 | 16 | 16 | 16 | 15 | 14 | 12 | 12 | 11 | 10 | 9 | 6 |
|----|----|----|----|----|----|----|----|----|----|----|----|----|
| IE | FI | LV | LT | LU | DK | FR | PL | BE | SI | PT | MT | IT |

# Trade and the economy

One of the EU's main aims is economic progress. Over the past 50 years, and especially since the 1980s, much has been done to break down the barriers between the EU's national economies and to create a single market where goods, people, money and services can move around freely. Trade between EU countries has greatly increased and, at the same time, the EU has become a major world trading power.

# How much does the EU produce?

The EU's gross domestic product (GDP) - i.e. the economy's output of goods and services - is steadily growing. With its enlargement from 15 to 25 countries, the EU's GDP is now about the same as that of the United States.

**GDP in billions of euro, 2003**

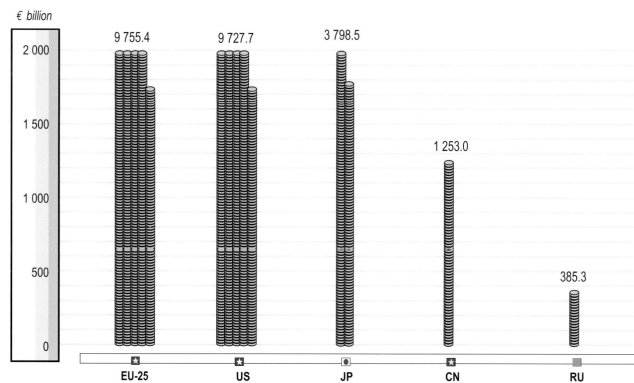

€ billion

| | EU-25 | US | JP | CN | RU |
|---|---|---|---|---|---|
| | 9 755.4 | 9 727.7 | 3 798.5 | 1 253.0 | 385.3 |

*Sources*: World Bank, Eurostat.

Although GDP in the new member states is on the whole smaller than in the older ones, it is growing at a very healthy rate - well above the EU-15 average. In all EU countries, over 60% of GDP is generated by the service sector (this includes things such as banking, tourism, transport and insurance). Industry and agriculture, although still important, have declined in economic importance in recent years.

**GDP in billions of euro, 2003**

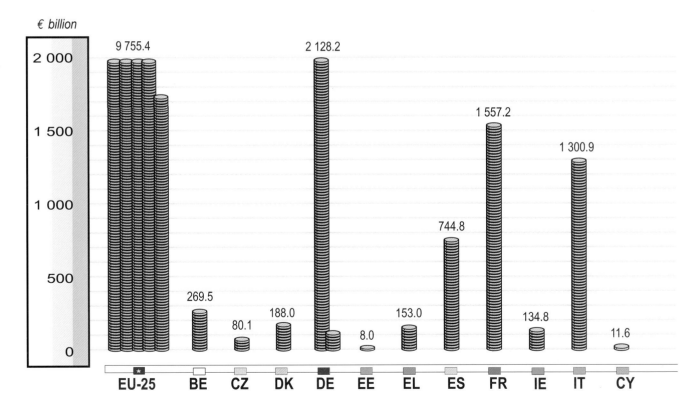

The figure for Austria is not fully comparable to the figures for other countries.

*Source:* Eurostat.

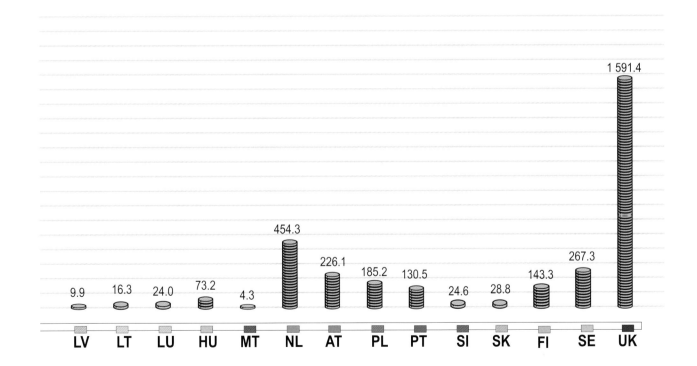

| LV | LT | LU | HU | MT | NL | AT | PL | PT | SI | SK | FI | SE | UK |
|----|----|----|----|----|----|----|----|----|----|----|----|----|----|
| 9.9 | 16.3 | 24.0 | 73.2 | 4.3 | 454.3 | 226.1 | 185.2 | 130.5 | 24.6 | 28.8 | 143.3 | 267.3 | 1 591.4 |

# The EU: a major trading power

Although the EU represents only 7% of the world's population, it accounts for approximately a fifth of global imports and exports. It is therefore a major trading power with an important role to play on the world stage.

Trade between EU countries accounts for two thirds of all EU trade, and it is vital to the economies of all the member states. It accounts for over half of all trade in each of the 25 countries, and in some cases it amounts to around 80% - as the graph shows.

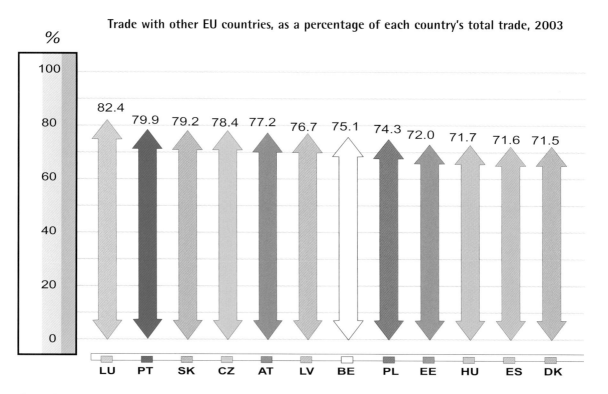

**Trade with other EU countries, as a percentage of each country's total trade, 2003**

| Country | % |
|---------|------|
| LU | 82.4 |
| PT | 79.9 |
| SK | 79.2 |
| CZ | 78.4 |
| AT | 77.2 |
| LV | 76.7 |
| BE | 75.1 |
| PL | 74.3 |
| EE | 72.0 |
| HU | 71.7 |
| ES | 71.6 |
| DK | 71.5 |

*Source*: Eurostat.

The single market has made trade between EU countries much easier as goods, services, capital and people can now move freely across national borders. It is also good news for consumers, who can shop around for the best bargains!

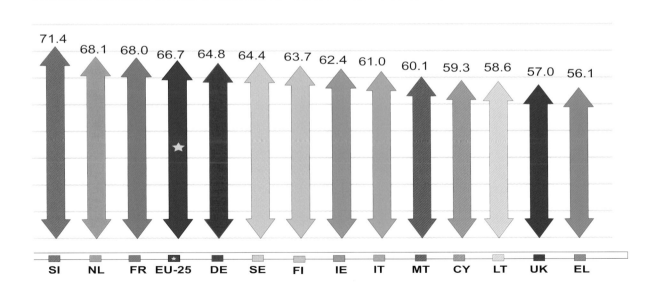

| SI | NL | FR | EU-25 | DE | SE | FI | IE | IT | MT | CY | LT | UK | EL |
|----|----|----|-------|----|----|----|----|----|----|----|----|----|----|
| 71.4 | 68.1 | 68.0 | 66.7 | 64.8 | 64.4 | 63.7 | 62.4 | 61.0 | 60.1 | 59.3 | 58.6 | 57.0 | 56.1 |

The EU is one of the main exporters of goods, as the graph below shows. The USA is the EU's biggest export market, and most of the goods entering the EU come from the USA. However, between 1999 and 2003, the EU's trade with China has more than doubled in value, and China is now the second biggest supplier of EU imports.

The EU is also an important trading partner for less developed countries, and this trade helps their economic growth. The EU is one of the biggest importers of agricultural products from less developed countries.

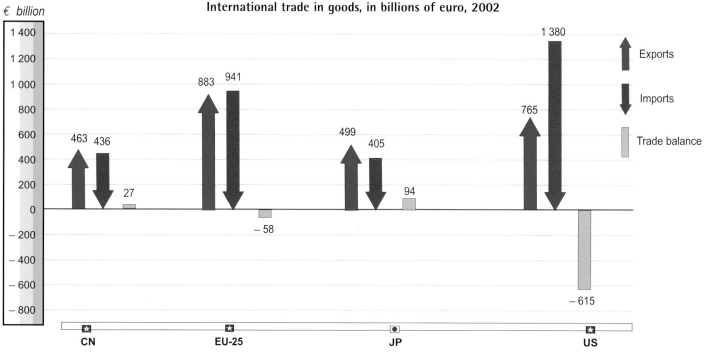

**International trade in goods, in billions of euro, 2002**

€ billion

Exports
Imports
Trade balance

CN: 463, 436, 27
EU-25: 883, 941, −58
JP: 499, 405, 94
US: 765, 1 380, −615

*Source*: Eurostat.

# The EU: fighting world poverty

Poverty is still a global problem, in spite of progress over recent decades. In 2001, in sub-Saharan Africa, 314 million people were living on less than a dollar a day. Even in Europe and central Asia, the figure was 18 million people.

The EU's status as a major trading power gives it great responsibility for fighting world poverty and promoting global development. It seeks to use its influence within the World Trade Organisation to ensure fair rules for world trade and to make globalisation benefit all nations, including the poorest. It is also the world's biggest donor of official development aid.

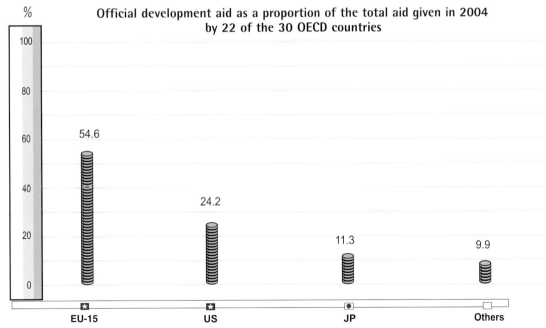

**Official development aid as a proportion of the total aid given in 2004 by 22 of the 30 OECD countries**

The data is preliminary.
The figure for the EU-15 includes aid managed by the EU institutions.
*Source*: OECD.

# Transport, energy and the environment

Transport and energy are vital to the EU economy. Europeans and the products they consume in ever increasing quantity and variety are carried across the continent by all modes of transport - but most of all by road.

As the economy grows, so does the demand for transport and energy. But this growth means increasing congestion and fuel consumption, which in turn create more pollution. These are Europe-wide problems that require Europe-wide solutions decided at EU level.

Sustainable development is a top priority for the EU, which takes environmental concerns into account in all its policy-making.

# Going places

Railways and inland waterways (i.e. rivers and canals), once so important for moving goods and passengers around Europe, now carry only a small percentage of the total. Three quarters of the European Union's freight now goes by road - as do more than three quarters of travellers in the EU.

Forecasts predict that road transport will remain by far the most important mode of travel for passengers and that air travel will continue to boom.

To ease congestion on the roads and improve the environment, the EU is encouraging people to travel by public transport and urging transport firms to move freight to trains, barges and ships. To tackle congestion at Europe's airports, the EU is creating a unified Europe-wide system of air traffic control (the 'single European sky').

**Use of four means of passenger transport in the EU-25 as a percentage of total passenger transport measured in passenger-kilometres, 2000, 2010 and 2030.**

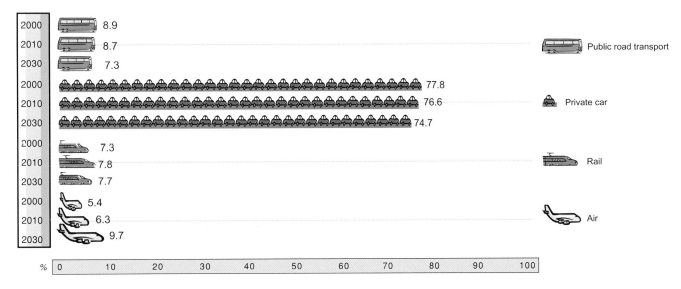

*Source*: European Commission.

# Power for the people

Two EU countries (Denmark and the United Kingdom) are net exporters of energy, thanks to their North Sea oil and gas reserves, but the EU as a whole is largely dependent on external suppliers of energy. In 2003, nearly a third of the EU's oil imports came from Russia. Overall, the EU imports about half the energy it consumes.

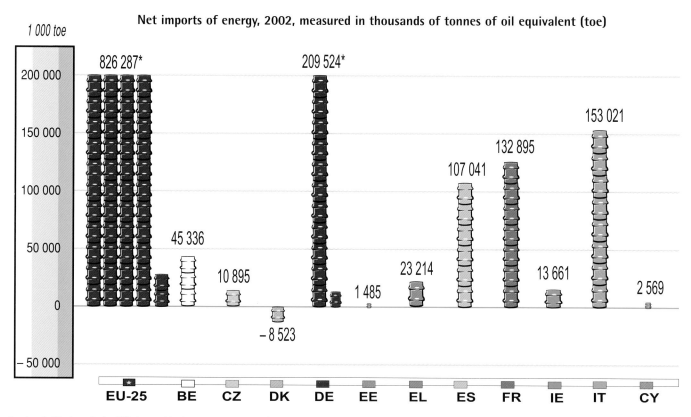

**Net imports of energy, 2002, measured in thousands of tonnes of oil equivalent (toe)**

*1 000 toe*

One toe is 10 gigacalories. This is roughly the energy content of one tonne of crude oil.
*Source*: Eurostat.

Dependence on imported energy, especially on oil, makes Europe vulnerable to international political crises, such as the oil crisis in 1973. So the EU is working hard to develop its own energy resources, including renewable resources.

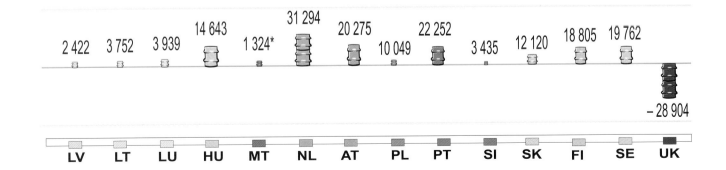

| LV | LT | LU | HU | MT | NL | AT | PL | PT | SI | SK | FI | SE | UK |
|----|----|----|----|----|----|----|----|----|----|----|----|----|----|
| 2 422 | 3 752 | 3 939 | 14 643 | 1 324* | 31 294 | 20 275 | 10 049 | 22 252 | 3 435 | 12 120 | 18 805 | 19 762 | – 28 904 |

Reserves of fossil fuels (coal, oil and natural gas) are limited, and burning them releases carbon dioxide into the atmosphere, contributing to global warming. So the EU is making a great effort to develop clean, renewable resources, such as wind, solar, hydroelectric and geothermal energy. The target for 2010 is to generate 21% of the EU's electricity from renewable sources.

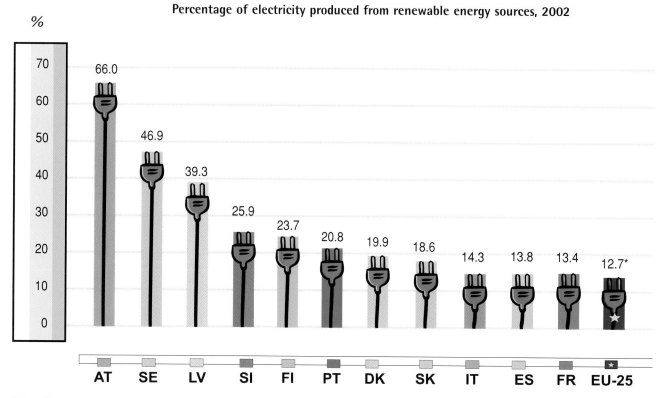

**Percentage of electricity produced from renewable energy sources, 2002**

%

| | AT | SE | LV | SI | FI | PT | DK | SK | IT | ES | FR | EU-25 |
|---|---|---|---|---|---|---|---|---|---|---|---|---|
| | 66.0 | 46.9 | 39.3 | 25.9 | 23.7 | 20.8 | 19.9 | 18.6 | 14.3 | 13.8 | 13.4 | 12.7* |

*Source*: Eurostat.

8.1*

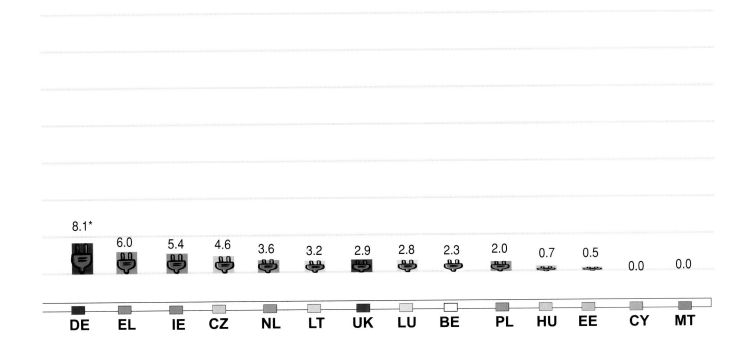

| 8.1* | 6.0 | 5.4 | 4.6 | 3.6 | 3.2 | 2.9 | 2.8 | 2.3 | 2.0 | 0.7 | 0.5 | 0.0 | 0.0 |
|------|-----|-----|-----|-----|-----|-----|-----|-----|-----|-----|-----|-----|-----|
| DE | EL | IE | CZ | NL | LT | UK | LU | BE | PL | HU | EE | CY | MT |

Household electricity prices vary considerably from one EU country to another, especially when national taxes are taken into account. To bring prices down, the EU is opening up national electricity markets to greater competition and, at the same time, developing trans-European networks that will deliver energy more cheaply and efficiently throughout the EU.

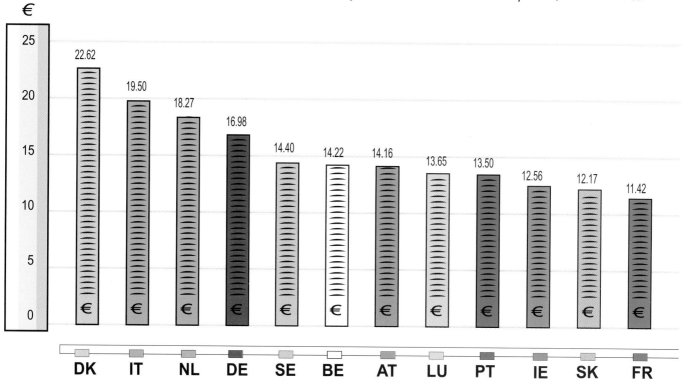

**Price of electricity for household use, in euro per 100 kilowatt-hour, January 2004, taxes included**

Source: Eurostat.

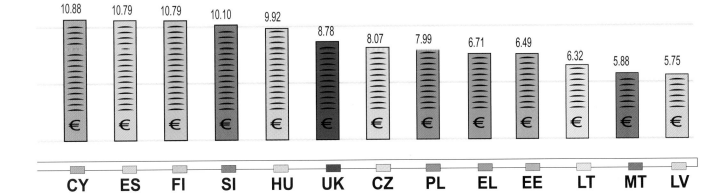

| CY | ES | FI | SI | HU | UK | CZ | PL | EL | EE | LT | MT | LV |
|------|------|------|------|------|------|------|------|------|------|------|------|------|
| 10.88 | 10.79 | 10.79 | 10.10 | 9.92 | 8.78 | 8.07 | 7.99 | 6.71 | 6.49 | 6.32 | 5.88 | 5.75 |

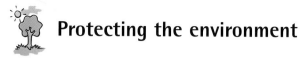

# Protecting the environment

Overall, Europe enjoys a temperate climate - which helps give it a very suitable environment for farming. But local conditions vary widely, from the Arctic north to the Mediterranean south, and from the milder climate of coastal regions to the hot summers and cold winters of inland areas.

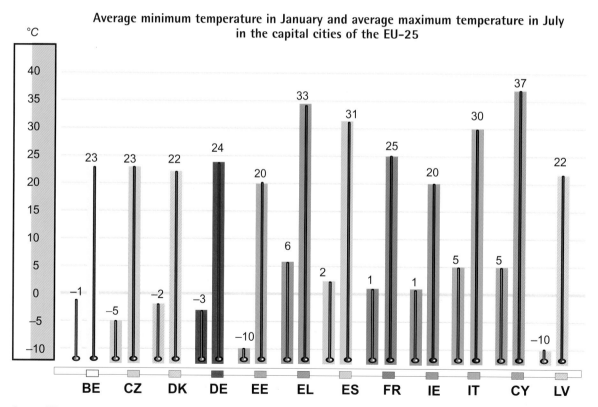

**Average minimum temperature in January and average maximum temperature in July in the capital cities of the EU-25**

Source: UK government Met Office.

Europe's climate contributes to its beautiful natural diversity and to its richly productive agriculture. However, these things are endangered by global climate change, which poses a serious threat to the planet as a whole. The EU is leading worldwide efforts to tackle this problem.

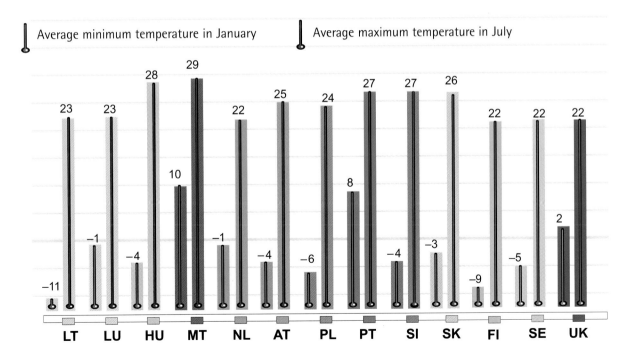

Average minimum temperature in January ┃ Average maximum temperature in July

| | LT | LU | HU | MT | NL | AT | PL | PT | SI | SK | FI | SE | UK |
|---|---|---|---|---|---|---|---|---|---|---|---|---|---|
| January | −11 | −1 | −4 | 10 | −1 | −4 | −6 | 8 | −4 | −3 | −9 | −5 | 2 |
| July | 23 | 23 | 28 | 29 | 22 | 25 | 24 | 27 | 27 | 26 | 22 | 22 | 22 |

Among the causes of global warming are the 'greenhouse gases' emitted into the atmosphere by motor vehicles, power plants, farms and factories. These gases include carbon dioxide ($CO_2$) and methane.

Under the Kyoto Protocol, which came into force in 2005, the EU-15 is committed to reducing greenhouse gas emissions by 8% (compared with 1990) by 2008-12. To reach this target, EU-15 countries have concluded a burden-sharing agreement under which a few of them can increase emissions while most of the economically more advanced member states reduce theirs. Eight countries that joined the EU in 2004 have individual emission reduction targets. Cyprus and Malta do not have a target.

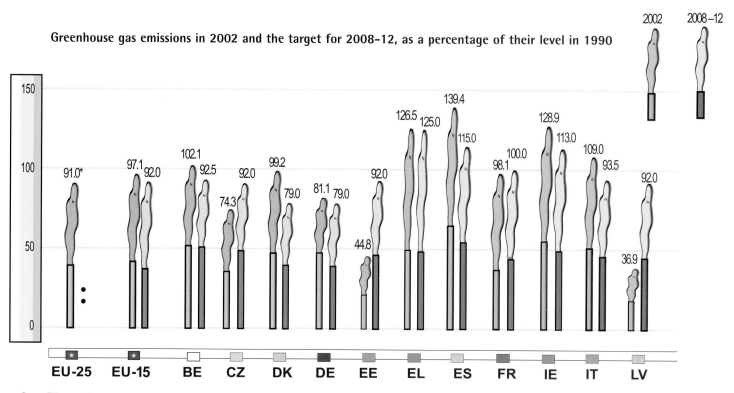

**Greenhouse gas emissions in 2002 and the target for 2008-12, as a percentage of their level in 1990**

Some EU countries have chosen a reference year other than 1990, and their reductions are calculated accordingly.
*Sources*: European Environment Agency, European Topic Centre on Air and Climate Change.

Emissions have not been reduced sufficiently, and determined action by all EU citizens is needed to meet the Kyoto targets.

The United States has not ratified the Kyoto Protocol.

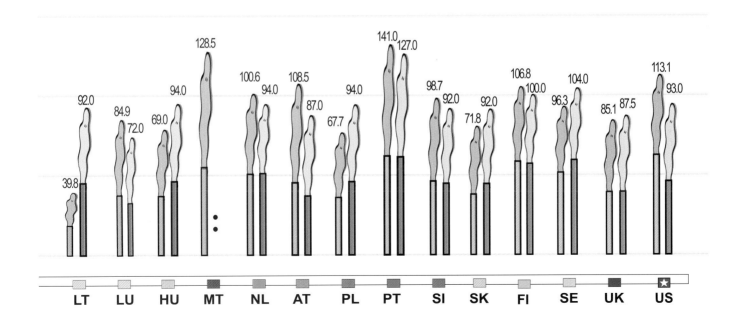

| LT | LU | HU | MT | NL | AT | PL | PT | SI | SK | FI | SE | UK | US |
|----|----|----|----|----|----|----|----|----|----|----|----|----|----|
| 39.8 / 92.0 | 84.9 / 72.0 | 69.0 / 94.0 | 128.5 | 100.6 / 94.0 | 108.5 / 87.0 | 67.7 / 94.0 | 141.0 / 127.0 | 98.7 / 92.0 | 71.8 / 92.0 | 106.8 / 100.0 | 96.3 / 104.0 | 85.1 / 87.5 | 113.1 / 93.0 |

# Europeans living together

Increasingly, EU citizens are getting to know one another and developing their sense of belonging together as Europeans - though not all are enthusiastic about the EU. Many spend their holidays in another European country, and increasing numbers of people go to study or work abroad, thanks to freedom of movement within the EU. Also, a high percentage of European school pupils learn at least one European language besides their own.

# Happy Europeans with shared concerns

In a Eurobarometer survey carried out in autumn 2004, eight out of every ten EU citizens said they were fairly or very satisfied with their life, and most are optimistic about the future. The 'very satisfied' percentage was 23%, compared with 19 % in autumn surveys in 2002 and 2003.

The number of people who say they are not at all satisfied has, for the past decade, remained relatively small at 4%.

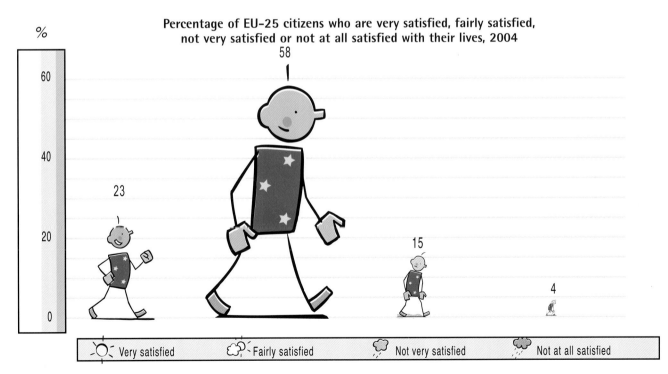

**Percentage of EU-25 citizens who are very satisfied, fairly satisfied, not very satisfied or not at all satisfied with their lives, 2004**

%

58

23

15

4

| Very satisfied | Fairly satisfied | Not very satisfied | Not at all satisfied |

*Source*: Eurobarometer.

Although generally happy with their life, Europeans do have concerns and worries. Three out of every four people were concerned about unemployment and the economic situation, identifying these as the two most important issues facing their country. Only 16% felt that terrorism was one of the top two issues.

Although results vary from country to country, reflecting the diversity of cultures and opinions in the EU, the survey shows that EU citizens share many common concerns.

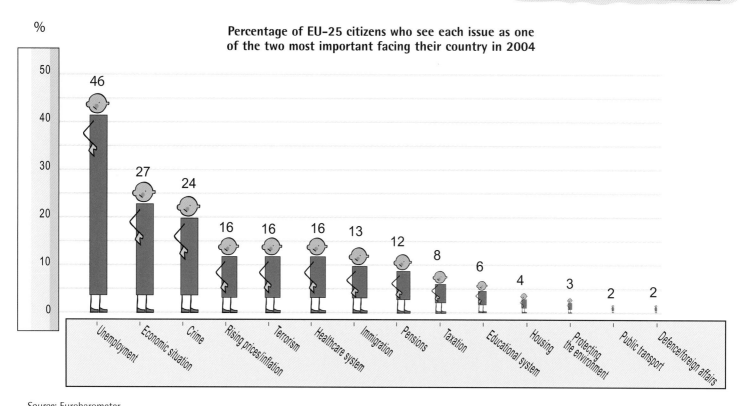

%

**Percentage of EU-25 citizens who see each issue as one of the two most important facing their country in 2004**

Unemployment 46
Economic situation 27
Crime 24
Rising prices/inflation 16
Terrorism 16
Healthcare system 16
Immigration 13
Pensions 12
Taxation 8
Educational system 6
Housing 4
Protecting the environment 3
Public transport 2
Defence/foreign affairs 2

*Source*: Eurobarometer.

# Studying together

Increasing numbers of young people are following educational courses in European countries other than their home country. This is largely thanks to EU schemes such as the Erasmus programme, which provides mobility in Europe for students and teachers. More than a million students have taken part in it since it began in 1987.

This scheme has now gone global with the launch, in 2004, of Erasmus Mundus.

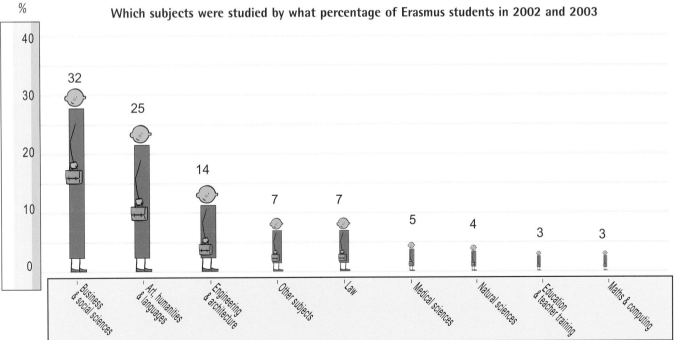

%

**Which subjects were studied by what percentage of Erasmus students in 2002 and 2003**

- Business & social sciences: 32
- Art, humanities & languages: 25
- Engineering & architecture: 14
- Other subjects: 7
- Law: 7
- Medical sciences: 5
- Natural sciences: 4
- Education & teacher training: 3
- Maths & computing: 3

*Source*: European Commission.

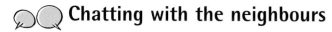# Chatting with the neighbours

According to a Eurobarometer survey, more than half of the people in the EU-15 in 2001 could speak at least one European language besides their own. The languages most commonly used by non-native speakers are English, French and German. Russian is also widely spoken in the 10 countries that joined the EU in 2004.

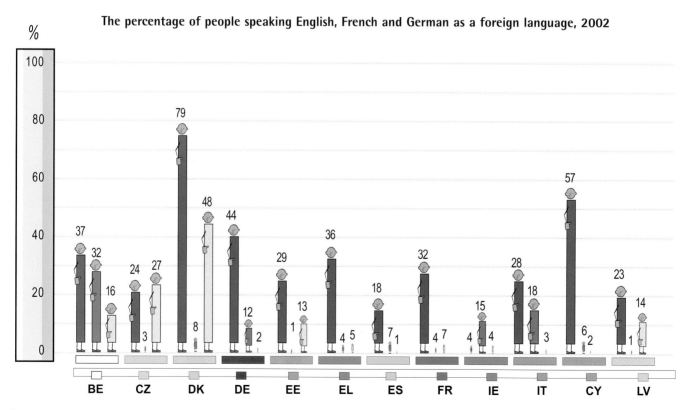

The percentage of people speaking English, French and German as a foreign language, 2002

*Source*: European Commission.

Being able to hold a conversation in a foreign language is useful for many purposes - studying abroad, travel, business contacts and international friendship - and it opens up all sorts of job opportunities. That's why the EU is encouraging all its citizens to learn two languages in addition to their mother tongue.

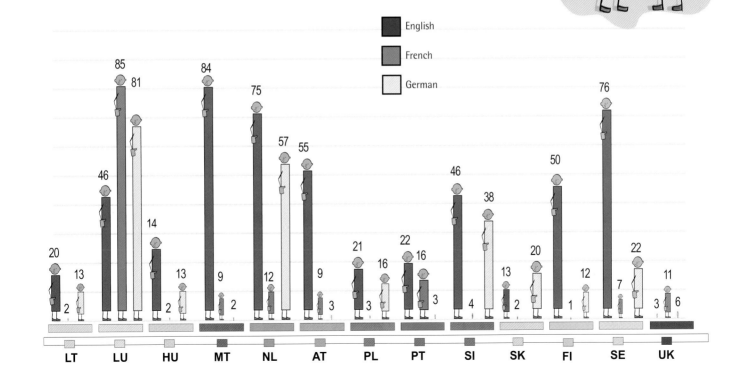

## 👍 👎 Supporters or sceptics?

Public support for the EU varies from country to country and fluctuates over time. According to a recent Eurobarometer survey, approval of EU membership is strongest in countries that are longstanding members of the EU. The jury is still out in many of the countries that joined in 2004.

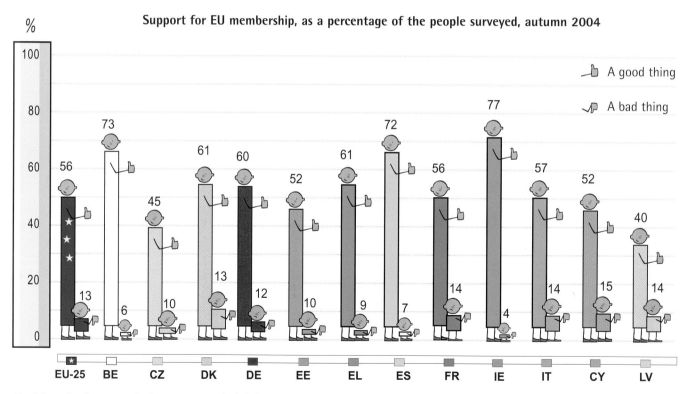

**Support for EU membership, as a percentage of the people surveyed, autumn 2004**

%

A good thing

A bad thing

EU-25: 56, 13
BE: 73, 6
CZ: 45, 10
DK: 61, 13
DE: 60, 12
EE: 52, 10
EL: 61, 9
ES: 72, 7
FR: 56, 14
IE: 77, 4
IT: 57, 14
CY: 52, 15
LV: 40, 14

'Don't knows' and non-committal answers are not included.

*Source*: Eurobarometer.

The country with the least public enthusiasm for the EU is the United Kingdom, which has a notably 'Euro-sceptic' press. Support for the European Union is strongest in Luxembourg - a small country with a high standard of living, and one of the original six member states.

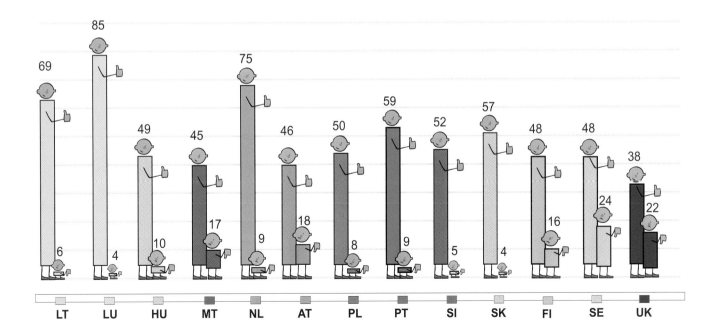

| LT | LU | HU | MT | NL | AT | PL | PT | SI | SK | FI | SE | UK |
|----|----|----|----|----|----|----|----|----|----|----|----|----|
| 69 | 85 | 49 | 45 | 75 | 46 | 50 | 59 | 52 | 57 | 48 | 48 | 38 |
| 6  | 4  | 10 | 17 | 9  | 18 | 8  | 9  | 5  | 4  | 16 | 24 | 22 |

# The candidate countries

If a country has applied to join the European Union and its application has been officially accepted, it is known as a 'candidate country'. At present there are four candidate countries: Bulgaria, Croatia, Romania and Turkey.

Before a candidate country can join the EU it must have a stable system of democratic government, and institutions that ensure the rule of law and respect for human rights. It must also have a functioning and competitive market economy and an administration capable of implementing EU laws and policies. The specific membership terms for each country are worked out in negotiations with the European Commission.

Two of the candidates (Bulgaria and Romania) are completing membership negotiations and are on track to join the EU in 2007.

# How big are they and how many people live there?

The candidate countries range in size from Croatia (smallest) to Turkey (largest).
If all these four countries joined the EU, this would boost its present population by over 100 million - an increase of around 23%.

**Surface area, in thousands of square kilometres**

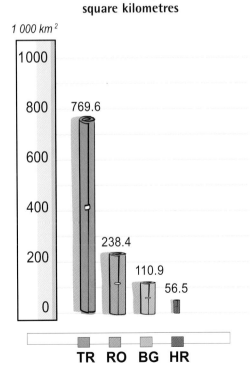

*1 000 km²*

- 769.6
- 238.4
- 110.9
- 56.5

TR RO BG HR

**Population in 2004, measured in millions of people**

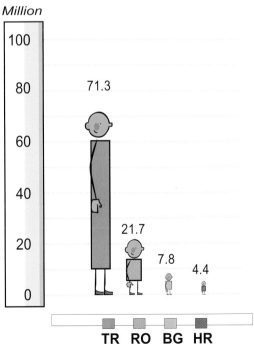

*Million*

- 71.3
- 21.7
- 7.8
- 4.4

TR RO BG HR

*Source*: European Commission.

Figures for Croatia are for 2003.
*Source*: Eurostat.

# How wealthy are they?

When you compare their GDP in PPS per inhabitant, the candidate countries are on the whole less wealthy than the EU countries. However, Croatia - at 45% of the EU-25 average figure - is wealthier than the poorest current EU member (Latvia: 41%).

**GDP in PPS per inhabitant, 2003, as a percentage of the EU-25 average**

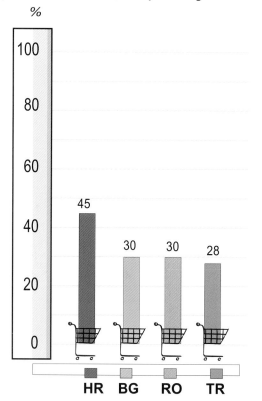

%

100

80

60

45

40

30    30    28

20

0

**HR   BG   RO   TR**

*Source*: Eurostat.

# People at work

Economic reforms in recent years have brought great changes in the candidate countries, helping create new jobs. Employment rates in all the candidate countries are lower than the EU-25 average, but Bulgaria, Croatia and Romania all have higher rates than Poland (the EU country with the lowest level of employment in 2003).

In the candidate countries as in the EU-25, services (including tourism) are an important part of the economy. However, in Bulgaria, Romania and Turkey, agriculture employs a much greater proportion of the population than in the EU-25.

## Employment rate, 2003

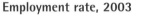

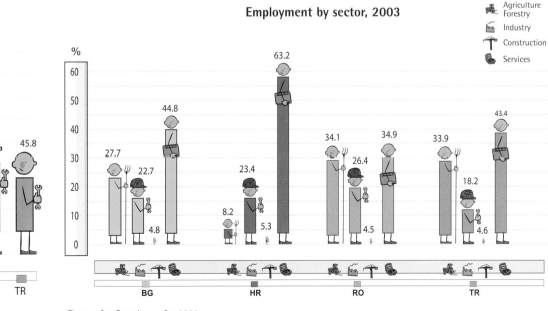

## Employment by sector, 2003

Agriculture Forestry
Industry
Construction
Services

Figures for Croatia are for 2002.
*Sources*: Eurostat, labour force survey, annual average.

Figures for Croatia are for 2002.
*Source*: European Commission.

 # Enthusiastic Europeans?

In autumn 2004, a Eurobarometer survey asked a representative sample of people in the candidate countries whether EU membership will be a good or bad thing for their country. In three of the countries, a clear majority believes EU membership will be a good thing but in Croatia opinion is much more evenly divided.

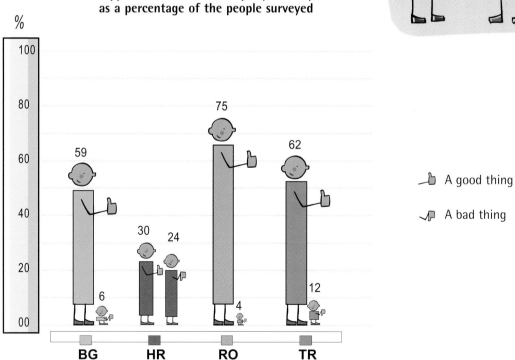

**Support for EU membership, by country, as a percentage of the people surveyed**

%

- 100
- 80
- 60
- 40
- 20
- 00

59 — BG
30 | 24 — HR
75 | 4 — RO
62 | 12 — TR

6

A good thing

A bad thing

'Don't knows' and non-committal answers are not included.

*Source*: Eurobarometer.

# A friendly neighbourhood

EU enlargement in 2004-07 is uniting a once-divided continent and creating a wider area of stability and prosperity in Europe. An area where democracy and the rule of law are secure and human rights are respected.

But the European Union does not want peace, democracy, stability and prosperity to stop at its frontiers. It does not want Europe to be divided yet again - this time by barriers between itself and its neighbours! So the EU is forging close ties with the countries on its borders (Russia, Belarus, Ukraine, Moldova, the Caucasus and Balkan regions) and with a wider circle of friends in the Middle East and North Africa.

By working constructively with all these countries on political as well as economic issues, and by giving them easy access to its huge single market, the EU aims to spread prosperity, stability and democratic progress throughout its neighbourhood. With the Balkan countries, the European Union has special 'association agreements' designed to pave the way for their eventual EU membership.

Over the period 2000–06, enlargement will have cost the EU only about a thousandth of its annual GDP. This is a tiny price to pay for the benefits of a united Europe and a more stable world.

European Commission

**Key facts and figures
about Europe and the Europeans**

Luxembourg: Office for Official Publications of the European Communities

2005 – 79 p. – 24.5 x 16.2 cm

ISBN 92-894-9551-0

**Summary**

The European Union (EU), with 25 member countries, covers a large part of the continent of Europe. When two more countries join in 2007, the EU will have a population of nearly half a billion.

The European Union aims to be a fair and caring society. All EU countries are committed to peace, democracy, the rule of law and respect for human rights, and they work together to promote these values in the wider world.

To become more competitive and prosperous, the EU is creating new and better jobs and giving its citizens new skills. In partnership with its near neighbours, the EU is working to spread prosperity and democratic progress beyond its borders.

Using charts, graphs and entertaining illustrations, this booklet sets out the basic facts and figures about the European Union. It draws interesting comparisons between its member states and, sometimes, with other major economies.

The countries that are candidates for EU membership are also included, in a separate section.